the leading

EDGE

LEARNING TO LEAD THE INTERSTATES WAY

the leading
EDGE

LEARNING TO LEAD THE INTERSTATES WAY

A collection of blog posts written by the
Interstates Senior Leadership Team

THRONE
PUBLISHING GROUP

INTERSTATES

Throne Publishing Group
2329 N Career Ave #215
Sioux Falls, SD 57107
ThronePG.com

TABLE OF CONTENTS

PART FOUR: SERVING CLIENTS

PART FIVE: LEADING PEOPLE

FOREWORD

The Interstates Way is more than a quick catchphrase or simple slogan. It's a belief system, a set of values, and a philosophy to approaching business. But it's also more than that. The Interstates Way is a guide that directs how our organization functions at every level.

At Interstates, we're proud of the culture we've created for our organization. That culture is centralized around a collective understanding and approach to leadership. This approach to leadership and people development is part of what makes us who we are. Serving others and equipping them to succeed is what makes up an Interstates leader.

Great leadership at Interstates is fostered in many ways. The champion of this leadership development, however, comes in the form of an internal training curriculum known as *Excellence in Leadership* (EIL). EIL provides a blueprint for success for our organization and the individuals herein. The principles of the Leadership Model explained in this book are the framework on which that blueprint was created.

The EIL program has several tiers that our leaders advance through. In the more advanced sessions, our EIL cohorts are often entrusted with larger enterprise initiatives and projects. These projects are sponsored by the Senior Leadership team, and the book you're holding is the direct result of one of them.

A familiar graphic says it well when describing an exchange between two members of an organization's leadership team. One employee opens the conversation asking, "What happens if we invest in our people and they choose to leave?" A short but immediate response comes from the other participant: "What happens if we don't and they choose to stay?"

It's a simple exchange but it holds as true today as it ever has. At Interstates we have no interest in finding out the answer to the latter question. And you shouldn't either.

The Senior Leadership team at Interstates created a Leadership Model that captures The Interstates Way. We believe it honors our past leaders and, more importantly, sets the direction for the leadership development of current and future Interstates leaders. Our vision is that this model will help you reach your potential.

It's important to view the model from an individual and a team perspective. Individually, all leaders can use the model to candidly reflect and assess their own strengths and weaknesses. The insight gained from that reflection will enable them to be deliberate about their development as leaders. It moves to a team perspective when leaders have the courage to share their self-assessments and development plans with others. This creates an opportunity for an exchange of feedback and fosters the creation of a community that accelerates learning and development for all involved.

Our leadership teams have adopted a philosophy that permeates our entire organization. Everyone can be a leader because everyone can serve. Regardless of your position or authority, all team members are leaders. And it is the responsibility of those in existing leadership roles to train and nurture their colleagues and team members to grow, expand their own leadership capacity, and take on new responsibilities themselves.

You can do the same. For your team, for your family, for your church or community group. Surround yourself with great team members and turn every one of them into a leader by first choosing to serve them. Invest in them from both a personal and professional standpoint. Equip them with the skills and tools needed to most effectively do their job and fulfill their purpose.

This book is a collection of blog posts from the Senior Leadership team at Interstates. Use them to challenge yourself, your beliefs, and your team in various areas of leadership. These blog posts and many others can be found on The Leading Edge blog.

It all starts with you. Yes, you. Here's to leading The Interstates Way.

The Excellence In Leadership 3 Peer Group
August 1, 2016

INTRODUCTION: LEADERSHIP THE INTERSTATES WAY

Preserve "The Interstates Way" – that is why we have the Leadership Model and why you have this book in front of you. As you go through this book, read it with a sharp and curious eye. We don't want you to accept it blindly. We want you to think and talk about it, to look for ways to apply it, challenge it, and, most importantly, make it yours. That is the only way we can ensure The Interstates Way passes from one leader to another and from one generation to the next.

PRESERVE THE INTERSTATES WAY

Our culture and the way we lead is changing and always will. We want to put a stake in the ground on a few things that should not change. We believe this because they are foundational pieces of our organization. These include who we have been, who we are, and who we want to be in the future. The model itself captures the *letter* of The Interstates Way. Understanding the *essence* of The Interstates Way is about how you live out the Leadership Model. Living The Interstates Way is a choice, a perspective to how you lead. It means leaning on servant leadership and is the most rewarding part of leading.

We have been blessed to work at Interstates because of the opportunities provided and the people who have invested in us. We truly believe we are better businessmen and -women, leaders, and, more importantly, better people because of the culture at Interstates. We want to enable the next generations of Interstates Leaders to have this same opportunity. We also want to set the direction for succession planning and leadership development.

LEADERSHIP SUCCESSION

When the Leadership Model was developed, our Senior Leadership Team was made up of five leaders: Larry Den Herder, Scott Peterson, Jack Woelber, Dave Crumrine, and Doug Post. This team did not ease into leadership succession planning. The group was forced into a dramatic ownership and leadership transition. During this time we faced an unsteady economy as a result of the 9/11 attacks and also lost a large project and one of our best clients to a buyout. In a six-month period we faced all of those items along with Darrel Ramhorst's retirement and the death of our forty-eight-year-old CEO, Jim Franken. These were tough and challenging times to be sure. It also provided an opportunity for this Senior Leadership Team to quickly bond and build trust, and the events acted as a catalyst for our approach to leadership development.

As we approached the next transition in ownership and leadership, we wanted to be purposeful. This group invested a great deal of time and energy into crafting the Leadership Model outlined in this book. We designed the model to help Interstates employees develop as leaders and to guide the organization through succession planning. Additionally, we use it as a tool to evaluate what we are great at, what we are good at, and what we struggle with. We evaluated each other against the model and against the current and future needs of the company. This Senior Leadership Team was, and continues to be, a strong and close-knit group. The process of developing and using this model made us stronger and drew us closer as a team. Because we understood more about each other we became more aligned and found ways to support each other at a deeper level. Having the Leadership Model was one of the keys that guided us through our CEO succession process when Larry announced his plans to retire.

LEADERSHIP DEVELOPMENT

As leaders take on more responsibility, they actually receive less feedback and less investment from others in their own development. A leader that does not have a model or a process of development is at huge risk of plateauing or regressing as a leader. Therefore, Senior Leaders must always look for ways to obtain feedback, evaluate their development and performance, and have a development plan. This also sets the expectation that all leaders must be continually developing themselves and others.

DEVELOPMENT AND PURPOSE OF THE MODEL

The development of this Leadership Model was a twelve-month journey. We engaged external consultants who were experts in organizational and leadership development through the process.

During this time, we researched several different Leadership Models and studied some of them in depth. We purposely set aside the model several times in order to let it sink in and identify what really fit us. Ultimately, this helped us discern what resonated and what did not – what was truly The Interstates Way. We also asked for feedback from shareholders as well as other internal and external leaders. What has become the Interstates Leadership Model is the result of a collaborative effort, an effort that is stronger because of the breadth and depth of leadership that came together to craft it.

Our hope is that the essence of the Interstates Leadership Model never changes, although the words and concepts within the model may be revised and updated as time passes. The model articulates who we are, how we lead, and why we lead the way we do. It is the culmination of what an Interstates leader aspires to embody.

The bottom line is that our employees are the key. They are the heart and soul of Interstates. As leaders, it is our responsibility to identify opportunities to give our people the chance to be challenged, to grow, and to do more than they ever thought possible.

The Senior Leadership Team has been very blessed, and one of our primary responsibilities will always be to steward this blessing well. Now, we invite you to join us and every Interstates leader who has gone before to lead The Interstates Way!

OUR LEADERSHIP HERITAGE, PHILOSOPHY, AND CULTURE

At Interstates, we have a rich heritage of strong leaders with big vision. From our founder's tenacious entrepreneurial spirit to Darrel Ramhorst's unique teaching gift, our leadership pedigree is diverse in its scope. Below are just a few of the keystone leaders who helped make Interstates the company it is today.

JOHN A. FRANKEN

Our founder was John A. Franken. He was 100 percent entrepreneur, and he had a knack for seeing an opportunity and going all in on it, whether it was a wise move or not. That confidence and swagger was both contagious and scary. It has also become part of our DNA – we love the challenges, the tough projects, and doing things that most people thought were impossible. That attitude leaked into our early marketing slogan: "The difficult we do immediately. The impossible takes a little longer."

JIM FRANKEN

Jim Franken was John's son and became CEO in 1995. He grew up in the organization, filling many different roles throughout his tenure. Jim served as an estimator, worked in purchasing, and also business development. Although his tenure as CEO was short (1995–2001), his passion for investing in leadership development and building a vision had an immeasurable impact on Interstates and our culture. He enjoyed working with leaders to "help them help themselves," which is one version of his personal mission statement. Jim wanted the company and each of its leaders to have a vision for the future, a vision that would provide guidance and motivation.

DARREL RAMHORST

Darrel Ramhorst was Interstates' first engineer, professional engineer (PE), and president of Interstates engineering. Darrel's passion was teaching people. He recognized the need for both leadership and technical training for team members and acted on that need. During his time with Interstates, he invested thousands of hours in training drafters, engineers, journeymen, electricians, and leaders. He could see the potential in people and loved finding the best way to help people learn. It is in honor of his commitment to developing people that our Sioux Center office houses a large conference and training room called the Ramhorst Training Center.

LARRY DEN HERDER

Larry Den Herder started as a high school intern and retired as Interstates CEO in 2014. During Larry's tenure, he had two major focus areas. For the first thirty years, he led our project delivery team and focused on delivering results to our clients. During the last fifteen years, he focused on understanding our clients' needs and building relationships with them. These relationships were key to Interstates' growth and success and set a great example for the whole company to follow.

JOHN DEZEEUW

John DeZeeuw was the CFO of Interstates from the inception of the company through the year 1997. His quiet leadership was the perfect balance to John A's hard-charging leadership. He helped set the tone for quality, professionalism, and, most importantly, doing the right thing. John had a well-hidden but very caring heart.

Through the years, Interstates has been fortunate to have had many great leaders. They have all brought their unique gifts and talents. Each one has made a huge contribution by leading projects, developing other leaders, landing work, investing in people, instilling a strong culture, or reinforcing our core values. The bottom line is that they paved a path and helped create The Interstates Way.

ENDURING COMPANY

The Senior Leadership Team truly wants Interstates to be an enduring company. We believe the best way to do this is by aligning our core ideology, ownership philosophy, and leadership philosophy.

LIVING OUT OUR CORE IDEOLOGY

Interstates' core ideology gives us direction, motivates us, and provides guidance. Our core values are about how we support each other and treat others, both internally and externally. More than a plaque on the wall, we strive to live these out each day.

> *Core Values: Building Relationships through*
> - *dependability;*
> - *integrity;*
> - *trust;*
> - *quality;*
> - *family.*

Our vision directs us to impact and serve our clients, vendors, and teammates by first seeking to truly understand their needs before making an attempt at a solution. We want to ensure we are delivering the exact results our customers are seeking, and in order to do so we must first understand their real needs.

> *Vision: Understanding Needs > Delivering Results*

We also believe that it's easiest for our leaders and employees alike to get behind that vision if they first understand our WHY. At Interstates, we are passionate about our WHY.

> *Why: At Interstates, we believe in . . .*
> - *providing opportunities for our people;*

- *making a difference for our clients;*
- *pursuing a better way.*

A LEADER-OWNED COMPANY PHILOSOPHY

Our ownership philosophy is designed to ensure Interstates is ridiculously in charge of its future, attract and retain leaders, and enable the leadership responsibilities to be passed from one generation of leaders to another.

We want Interstates to be a leader-owned company. This philosophy allows our leader-owners to balance the short term with the long term. In addition, actively leading gives those with an ownership stake a more well-rounded insight into the business, the culture, the clients, and the people. We believe this allows us to leverage servant leadership at Interstates and is a key element of The Interstates Way. The leader-owners are the stewards of the company and are responsible for leaving it in better shape related to areas like culture, finances, clients, internal processes, learning, and growth.

Owners buy in and sell their stock at book value. We constantly get pushback on this method. Good business leaders advise us that we are undervaluing Interstates, which is true. Every owner gets the benefit of buying in at the undervalued price. They normally receive great returns during their tenure. Then, they sell their stock at the undervalued price when they retire. It may not be a perfect system, but it fits Interstates best because it enables us to pass the company from one leadership generation to the next. This is a key element to becoming and maintaining an enduring company.

We have two types of stock ownership (A and B). The purpose of the A stock is as follows:

- Have a small number of shareholders that control a majority of the company to ensure the organization can move quickly in a crisis or to seize an opportunity.
- Make good long-term and short-term decisions with limited politics.
- Make good long-term decisions on the ownership structure.

The purpose of the B Stock is as follows:
- Retain and attract servant leaders.
- Give long-term opportunities to leaders.
- Help leaders grow their wealth.
- Bolster the sustainability of the company.
- Create a pipeline of potential A shareholders.

As of this writing, we have a total of thirty-eight shareholders between the two groups.

LEADERSHIP PHILOSOPHY: WORLDVIEW AND OUR CULTURE

We believe that our culture and values make us special and unique. It is the responsibility of the Senior Leadership Team to protect and live our core values, while nurturing and developing the culture toward our envisioned future. This role also needs to be balanced with being an advocate for our team members and being an advocate for our companies. All of this needs to happen with a long-term perspective of five to forty years. At times, we may need to choose between two or more good options.

Our worldview, our assumptions, and our desires about how challenges will be met and daily decisions will be made include the following:

1. We expect each leader to lead The Interstates Way.
2. We expect each team member to understand and commit to living our core ideology (Values, Vision, and our WHY).
3. A great team will be inclusive, not exclusive. We encourage team members to embrace similarities and differences in order to become a stronger and healthier team that can make a positive impact in our world.
4. We believe there is a greater purpose and calling in life that extends beyond our individual families and careers. Therefore, we encourage team members to develop a strong sense of personal mission. We also believe that all people are called to help and serve others so we need to remain humble and listen to the people speaking in our lives (i.e., team members, family, friends, vendors, clients, etc.).

PART ONE
LEADING STRATEGY

Having vision for an organization, crafting overall strategies, and effectively sharing those with the team are crucial skills for effective leaders. At Interstates, we equip our leaders with the necessary tools and skills to cast that vision, enable innovation, and motivate our team members. These are not simple suggestions for effective leadership; rather, they are challenges that our leaders must tackle and address on a daily basis.

CHAPTER ONE
INTERSTATES LEADERS ARE BOOK SMART AND STREET SMART

W e've seen it in the movies. The green lieutenant, fresh out of West Point, struggles leading his platoon until an old, crusty sergeant takes him under his wing and teaches him the ropes of the real world. The lieutenant is "book smart," the sergeant "street smart." By the end of the movie, the sergeant proudly watches a capable, confident lieutenant lead by practically applying his lessons on the battlefield.

Interstates leaders must also be book smart and street smart. At the end of the day, the result of our work is successfully built or operating industrial facilities. The result of our leadership is an organization that is built to last and operate in a tough, unforgiving marketplace.

Street-smart leaders know how businesses and people work. They know how to implement initiatives and run the business in a way that is practical and motivates people. They understand what it takes to meet client needs profitably, are aware of market forces and competitors that affect operations, and are able to adjust accordingly. They get things done with and for others.

My favorite example is our response to a Central Soya extraction explosion in the 1990s. Our team was well into the electrical installation work at the time of the disaster. And this wasn't just any project; it was in the heart of Indianapolis just a couple of miles from the Indianapolis Motor Speedway. Our crew had been working on site for a few months and was preparing for a shutdown and some rework in the extractor area. Then, one night, disaster struck. One issue built upon another and the Central Soya operators lost control of the extractor. Eventually, the facility began blowing hexane gas vapors into a public street. The situation grew more dangerous by the minute and culminated when a car passed through the cloud of vapors causing an explosion and a major fire to break out. This resulted in serious damage to both the plant and surrounding neighborhood homes.

Larry Den Herder didn't know how he could best help this key client, but that didn't keep him from trusting his gut and getting on a plane that very day. He wanted to go figure out what we could do as individuals and as an organization to make a difference at the site. Leaving at 3:30 a.m., a few short hours after finding out about the incident, he even beat some of the Central Soya leadership to the scene. Over the next weeks and months he, along with our field crew onsite, became an instrumental part of the client's recovery team. We learned a monumental lesson: When a customer has a problem, help them solve it. By doing this, we built a very long-lasting relationship with this customer.

Other street-smart examples of Interstates leadership include the Local Projects Group (LPG) kicking off its industrial growth by focusing on small, dirty jobs no one else wanted, and Larry driving our teams to proposal wins. Larry enjoyed digging in and figuring out how to get clients to award us projects. Imagine the negotiating, the scrappy tenacity, the hustle, and the awareness of client needs and budgets necessary to accomplish these wins.

Book-smart leaders are intelligent, continuous learners who comfortably deal with concepts and complexity. They shun easy answers and seek simplicity on the other side of complexity. For example, they see quality issues as more than a quick fix via a quality checklist and a training class. While these tactical steps may be necessary, book-smart leaders also examine hiring practices and organizational culture as potentially more fundamental causes of the problem. In other words, they think broadly and seek to understand the underlying system.

Systems thinking is all about the ability to see patterns of change and how parts affect the whole. Systems thinking skills enable leaders to see similarities between diverse areas of thought and practice, which they can then apply at Interstates.

This "book-smart" component, which is also immensely practical, deserves an aside as it has shaped fifteen years of leadership at Interstates. By way of definition, systems thinking can be defined as follows:

In his classic book, *The Fifth Discipline*, Peter Senge identifies eleven laws of systems thinking:[1]

1. *Today's problems often arise from yesterday's "solutions."* Thus, short-term solutions that shift problems from one part of a system somewhere else are ineffective. What's needed are changes in the system itself. For example, at Interstates, we believe

---

[1]As described in the book summary by summaries.com.

construction value increases when we leave a design-bid-build mental model for a design-build mentality.

2. *The easy way out almost guarantees long-term pain.* If the solution to a problem were obvious, wouldn't it already have been tried? Long-term systems thinking always avoids short cuts and focuses on developing effective systems instead. At Interstates, servant leaders take on the extra, needed effort to set systems up well so that their people benefit.

3. *Find the Levers: small changes can produce large results.* Systems have the effect of amplifying changes. Thus, small but well-focused changes can produce substantial, enduring changes – if they are the right changes in the first place.

4. *Avoid arbitrary boundaries.* Systems thinking requires looking at the entire organization and its underlying processes, irrespective of arbitrary organizational boundaries. That way important interactions can be factored in and studied rather than thinking, "It's someone else's problem." Often, the greatest gains in performance come when one part of the organization improves the way it interacts with another part. As leaders we must hold Interstates' business unit and department structures loosely by always remaining aware of the current state's pros and cons.

As far as the remaining seven laws ... well, you're going to have to read the book! I can't think of a better way to (1) learn essential systems thinking skills as well as (2) lead a learning organization via stewardship, designing the business, teaching, and harnessing creative tension.

CHAPTER TWO
INTERSTATES LEADERS MOVE FROM MUCK TO CLARITY

In his book *Leadership Is an Art*, Max De Pree wrote, "One of the key responsibilities of leadership is to define reality." Leaders determine the reality of where we are as a company and what challenges lie before us. Reality ultimately helps teams figure out what to pursue ... with clarity! Clarity is essential for performance, whether strategic or tactical. Without clarity, human beings wait, defer, and hedge. Almost none of us is immune to this phenomenon.

Creating clarity is a big job in most organizations, and the need for it is growing exponentially over time. The world is changing faster and faster, and our historical ways of dealing with it cannot keep up. Currently, the U.S. military is engaged in an effort to rewrite how they make decisions so that they can be effective in the quickly changing battlefields of today and tomorrow. Our challenges are similarly difficult, but, with committed leadership addressing the issue, we can be effective.

"Muck" is a term for what the world brings to us – complexity, change, struggles. Whether it is rational, emotional, or all in between, muck is complex and messy. Leaders need to engage in the muck and lead through it. Without this leadership, the team will struggle in many ways.

The first step in this process is to find clarity. Getting there, however, is often the hardest part of the performance journey. As Albert Einstein said, "If I had an hour to solve a problem, I'd spend fifty-five minutes thinking about the problem and five minutes thinking about solutions." As engineers, technicians, and project managers we often struggle in this area and want to hop into solution-mode too quickly. Why? Because we are good at solving problems. That's our job. The trap here is that we start by solving a problem that is not the true root of our challenge, often because it is the most obvious solution at that moment. Leaders need to resist this temptation and solve the root issue with a systems-thinking approach.

Clarity allows us to act together and with focus. It is the difference between a flashlight and a laser. When we use our limited energy on a specific problem, we can be extremely impactful. The clarity provides that difference. This doesn't mean we research forever or never act. There will always be uncertainty and risks to manage (and the leader is responsible for acknowledging these facts and presenting them to the team), but having the problem clearly defined sets the team up for true success.

A key idea that comes to light when discussing leadership is "the beauty of the AND." Jim Collins, author of *Good to Great*, and others have discussed this in their writings, and our Senior Team feels compelled to share that we shouldn't oversimplify problems. When we do this, we end up with a "we can do this OR we can do that" scenario. Our *Crucial Conversations* training shows us that this is a sucker's choice and it sets a team up to underperform. By looking for the best out of multiple options and merging them together, we are looking for the beauty of the AND. This is also called systems thinking and is an emerging piece of what Integrated Project Delivery (IPD) requires. We need to be exemplary in this area.

Systems thinking is what many in the manufacturing world have done to harness their potential. First, they break everything down into individual steps and optimize it into an assembly line. However, over the decades, in order to compete and thrive, they needed to reintegrate manufacturing, making individual steps and team members work together in harmony. This is like beautiful rhythmic dancing, not following steps on the floor while counting. This needs to be the evolution in our business as well.

Finally, to complete the move from muck to clarity, we must be able to make choices. We haven't been great at this step, and no good idea seems to go without attention here at Interstates. We need to excel at picking the brightest ideas and the strategies with the highest potential. Again, this will lead to clarity and focus, and through that, a lot of accomplishment in a rapidly changing world. Leaders must drive this process. They must lead their teams through realistic selection efforts and true assessments of their team's capacity. We must be honest and real.

Are you leveraging your leadership to achieve more clarity and less "muck"? From whatever level you are leading, are you setting your team up for success by driving for clarity?

CHAPTER THREE
INTERSTATES LEADERS ENABLE INNOVATION

How do innovation and change really happen? Like many things in organizational life, innovation and change require energy. Whether you envision a seed needing fertilizer or energy from the sun, innovation and change need nurturing. It could look like supporting someone with a passion, an idea they want to see flourish, or simply a need that pops up in the course of business. Entire organizations often do not, or cannot, create ideas spontaneously; they must be individually pushed, presented, or otherwise poked into the organization.

Even when good ideas are created and presented, organizational momentum can be the great killer of ideas. We are all fond of our routines and have grown used to how they work. Upsetting the status quo doesn't often seem to be the right thing to do. That is why leaders must be the agents of change. They need to be the advocates of change. This could look like promoting the why behind a change, supporting different thinking, or even allowing the questioning of tradition and sacred cows. If the idea can be sponsored into the organizational mindshare, the sponsor will need to lead the change that follows.

Ideas without implementation are simply daydreams. Referencing your early training, you have already learned that the manager inside of us likes to keep things predictable and performing at status quo. The leader within us is driven to promote the change required to win in the future. Knowing when it is time to drive innovation and change is the leader's task – perhaps one of the most important he or she carries. Without this trigger coming from leaders, change simply doesn't happen, and you risk missing out on significant advancements.

One familiar example of this at Interstates is the development of the prefabrication group, InterFab. The creation of this team and service offering has allowed for significant contributions to client projects, as well as providing a safe, controlled environment for construction tasks that would have otherwise been performed in the field. This simple innovation allows for additional work to be completed in less time while reducing the requirement of onsite personnel, in turn reducing the final project costs for our customers.

Step one of the change model we use at Interstates is understanding and increasing urgency. Leaders need to look for that urgency and realistically assess if the organization needs this change or not. Sometimes, urgency is hiding because the impact is off somewhere in the future, but these are often the important, and more difficult, changes to drive.

Many of us have seen people or organizations that seem devoid of an ability to change. How do you perceive them? Do you imagine they recognize this weakness from the inside of their own organization? This is the big difference. Are the organization's leaders seeing the need and acting on it?

After we recognize a need, leaders must have the skills and knowledge to help their teams pick the right change to pursue, all the way from building the right brainstorming team, offering a great challenge question, and continuing on through Kotter's 8-step change process.[2] In every change I have led over the years, if the initiative was struggling, I went back and looked at this change model. I could tell within minutes where I had gone wrong and where I needed to shore up the process. It was still difficult, and there was lots of work to do, but there is a reliable process for making change, and leaders must drive it.

From the beginning, Interstates has had more than its share of leaders who wanted to make change – to do things differently, to make things better in the pursuit of excellence. This is why one of the core ideas of our WHY statement is "Pursuing a Better Way." At Interstates, we have always believed this was our job to do. Not only is it the right thing to do for our clients and industry, it emotionally feeds and drives us. We derive energy and satisfaction from implementing change and doing so well.

This process takes energy. To make things happen in an expanding organization, we need leaders at every level to be looking for opportunities to innovate and then driving the change as well. We have invested in education and staff to build up innovation and alternative thinking, but we will always need leaders throughout the organization who see it as their role to ask the tough questions, to challenge the status quo, and to really drive toward a better way.

---

[2]http://www.kotterinternational.com/the-8-step-process-for-leading-change/

Thanks for being one of those leaders! Make sure you have put on your armor of change management and innovation knowledge. It makes for a powerful set of tools for conquering challenge and change.

CHAPTER FOUR
INTERSTATES LEADERS CAST VISION

Holocaust survivor Viktor Frankl shared that the single most significant factor for survival was a sense of future vision, a conviction that one still had important work to do. Vision is the ability to see beyond our present reality, to create, to invent what does not yet exist, and to become what we are not yet.

"Interstates leaders are tireless believers in people" is how I remember Jim Franken kicking off his vision for a new Interstates, which focused on leadership development. This was a startling change for a company previously focused almost exclusively on technical expertise. Through sharing his vision at company forums, leading us all through a book review of *The 21 Irrefutable Laws of Leadership* by John Maxwell, and by hiring non-technical leaders, Jim cast his vision for leadership at Interstates, and it became ours. After his untimely death, his direct reports were instrumental in continuing his vision through what we know today as our EIL series of courses.

Jim developed and shared a compelling vision for leadership at Interstates. He was persistent, always reminding us to lead better.

He was inspiring, convincing us that we could contribute more than we thought possible. He was motivating, driving growth like we hadn't been a part of before. In sum, great leaders cast a vision for their people so that

- they have a purpose larger than themselves;
- they know where they are going;
- they can create what doesn't yet exist;
- they are empowered to perform beyond their resources.

You do not need to be CEO to cast a compelling vision. Interstates leaders understand their team's current state and connect their department or project team's goals to the Interstates' WHY by making it practical for their people's day-to-day work. If you are a project manager, for example, consider beginning your project meetings with a discussion on how the team is making a difference for our clients on this project. You could also prompt the team with another question: "Are we really understanding their needs?" If you lead a department or a team, do your goals, training, and internal processes reflect a commitment to our vision?

I encourage you to frequently look beyond today to your picture of the future. Each day, make time to have one conversation or to take one step toward a better tomorrow.

PART TWO
LEADING OPERATIONS

E ven a great idea can fail if not properly executed and man-
aged. As a projects-based organization, we rely heavily on
effective operations to run our business. Appropriately setting direction, solving problems, and aligning resources are of the
utmost importance for today's leaders.

CHAPTER FIVE

INTERSTATES LEADERS SET DIRECTION

A common term in Interstates' *Excellence In Leadership* (EIL) course is Setting Direction. For those who have not yet been through EIL, one of the acronyms regularly used in our training is SAM. The "S" stands for setting direction, and it is one of the major tenets in the model Interstates uses when training employees on leadership.

Setting direction is critical. You may have heard the saying, "I'm their leader, which way did they go?" Most employees are more than willing to work hard, but without direction, you might not know which way they are going. Without direction, their work can lack motivation and be less beneficial to the organization. Similarly, a poor plan well executed still nets an unsatisfactory result. When clear direction is established, employees will display a heightened sense of purpose and can add more value by contributing their own ideas. When a leader fails in setting direction, employees can carry out a task but are often limited on the impact of their work.

Once you have determined a clear direction, proper communication is critical. Have you ever heard the phrase, "Just because I said it doesn't mean they heard it"? This is so true regarding setting direction. You may feel like you have laid out a clear direction for your team, but without confirmation and follow-up, it may have not been heard as you intended. Communicating the direction may take multiple efforts in different ways for your team to truly see the direction. Everyone learns and understands through different methods, and it is up to you to be sure you have done a good job of setting an understandable direction with your team. Having an effective rapport with your team and allowing them to feel comfortable asking clarifying questions can be a major asset in ensuring they understand the direction.

Another way to set clear direction is through the creation of goals and stretch goals. This format can paint a direction for the team to better understand. By having the team participate in setting those goals a leader can achieve greater buy-in. Similarly, the team members will more easily know and understand what they can do to help reach those goals. With everyone pulling in the same direction, with clarity, the chances of reaching your goals are much higher.

Sometimes there are multiple ways to get to the same destination. When setting direction, we need to take into consideration the resources we have available to us in time, energy, and money. Choosing the best way may not always be the least expensive or the quickest, but we need to determine if we can achieve our goals within the boundaries of our limited resources. If not, we may have to adjust our direction to achieve what we can within our budget or allotted timeframe.

One might wonder why setting direction is under the category of Leading Operations rather than Leading Strategy. Using

Interstates lingo, Leading Strategy involves casting a vision. Setting direction needs to align with that vision and strategy but refers more to leading operations than it does leading strategy. While these two things are closely related and need to reinforce each other, both are unique elements of leadership.

Setting direction is critical to leadership at Interstates. In our leadership training, we spend a lot of time and energy talking about and proper direction setting. My challenge to you is to consciously think about setting direction in a way that gets everyone pulling in the same direction with a common goal.

CHAPTER SIX
INTERSTATES LEADERS DELEGATE

Why delegate? Delegation is a crucial skill and practice for leaders at a company whose "Why Do We Exist?" statement includes "providing opportunities for our people" and whose core values emphasize building relationships by extending trust to others. We simply cannot live our core ideology if we do not delegate frequently, quickly, and clearly.

Good delegation allows Interstates' leaders to spend more of their time on fewer, more appropriate pursuits. It provides an opportunity to coach our people, giving them a chance to take on responsibility, learn new things, and grow their skills. In sum, it enables company growth and develops future leaders so that Interstates can be a company built to last.

I vividly remember how I felt when Darrel Ramhorst first asked me to lead a project for Interstates. I was excited, engaged, and felt ownership on that project. Today, it's our responsibility to frequently create similar opportunities for our people.

So when should you delegate? As soon as possible! When you're assigned a task or project, you need to make a decision as to whether or not you should delegate that task. If any of the above reasons for "why delegate?" apply to you, then delegate.

Quick decisions to delegate a task or project are essential, since delegating well takes time and effort. You will need to define what it is you really want, find someone to do the work, and leave time for reviews and adjustments since you are still accountable for the assignment.

Good leaders also take chances by over-delegating. Give people an opportunity to show you what they can do. As long as you are there to support them, they will be able to either accomplish the task or learn from the situation. Either way, everyone is better off. The next time you delegate, reflect on what good and bad delegation looks like before you implement.

Good delegation can be reduced to three key steps. First, clearly defining the scope, schedule, and budget of the assignment. Second, physically delegating the task with the support of the delegatee's manager. Third, completing the first two steps with the delegatee's specific situation in mind. This third step is critical. If you have attended EIL, you're familiar with Situational Delegation. To delegate well, remember it is your job to assess the delegatee's experience, knowledge, willingness, capacity, and motivation regarding the task. This helps you decide if you should direct, coach, support, or delegate.

Remember that first project I mentioned? Sometime later, it became obvious that Darrel had been walking beside me the whole way. Behind the scenes, he enlisted the client to be patient with a young project manager. He quietly coached me on client expectations and The Interstates Way. He lived **UNDERSTANDING NEEDS ▶ DELIVERING RESULTS** long before it was our stated vision. That's delegating.

CHAPTER SEVEN
INTERSTATES LEADERS SOLVE PROBLEMS

Why did the Interstates Senior Team decide to put something so obvious in its Leadership Model? Almost any business is rife with problems, and leaders are often called upon to solve them. If you succeed at solving one problem, there are often many other problems following along closely that will also require your attention. Although we spend a lot of time on problems, the truth is that we aren't very good at escaping some of the historical traps of problem solving.

The reason we chose to elevate the topic of solving problems is that it differs greatly from temporarily solving the symptoms of problems. Strong leaders need to have both the wisdom to identify the most essential problems to solve (there are always more than we can work on at one time) and the fortitude to work on the root cause of a problem. Working on the symptoms of a problem is like taking an aspirin every four hours to alleviate the pain of an infection. If you define the pain itself as the problem, you can solve it temporarily with a pain reliever. This is not an uncommon response by teams with urgent deadlines and limited resources. What you can't do with a pain reliever is prevent the pain from coming back. That takes a real cure, solving the problem from a systems-thinking perspective.

Real leadership requires we dig down past the quick and dirty solutions and find the root cause of problems. We must be suspicious of obvious solutions. To do this, we must help our people move past the urgent and help them truly see what is going on. We have learned much about Lean practices in our leadership journey. Many of the tools in Lean are built around the need to make the process visual and, in doing so, allowing the players to see what is really happening. This leads to much stronger problem-solving abilities that can effectively put challenges behind us – not to mention saving lots of trips to the store for more pain reliever.

As Interstates' leaders build their skills and knowledge around strong problem solving, others in the organization call on them for these abilities. These leaders become valued experts at facilitating problem solving; in the process, they also teach others the process to become better problem solvers themselves. Helping people build broad problem-solving skills is the real power here.

A controversial practice at Interstates seems to be bringing in non-experts to help solve problems. This is at odds with our natural inclination to use a room full of the most informed technical experts in an area. I'm not quite sure where this inclination comes from, but it is often a dominant idea we all have early in our careers. As Albert Einstein said, "We cannot solve our problems with the same thinking we used when we created them." This is why true problem-solving skills and coaching are required in our world. Perspective is the secret sauce of problem solving, and we must seek out non-traditional perspectives on a problem so we can expose our mental models and potentially flawed assumptions. Only then can we find the solutions we really need. Assumption-busting is the fuel of problem solving and innovation, and it is the key for Interstates to become a learning organization.

Problem-solving activity is common. Great problem solving, much less so. Leading The Interstates Way means digging deep enough to get it right!

CHAPTER EIGHT

INTERSTATES LEADERS DRIVE RESULTS DIRECTLY AND INDIRECTLY

W hy is driving results, both directly and indirectly, important to leadership? As you think about this topic, say it in your mind with two different emphases. First, DRIVING RESULTS directly and indirectly, and second, driving results DIRECTLY and INDIRECTLY.

When most people read this, on the surface, focusing our emphasis on driving results probably makes a lot of sense. However, it is good to remember that activity is different from results. There are times when someone can drive a lot of activity and yet not reach the desired result. That is why, when setting direction, it is good to have measureable goals to ensure you are reaching the desired result, rather than just feeling good about all the activity.

What kind of person does it take to reach those desired results? It takes someone who is action oriented and willing to take the initiative to dive in and make things happen. It also helps if the person is willing to take on a challenge. As discussed in chapter 2, many aspects of leadership start out a little fuzzy and, without the desire to take on a challenge, you can run out of steam pretty quickly. Through that fuzziness, you have to be able to remove the barriers and roadblocks by keeping the end in mind. Once you have reached your goal, it is good to reflect on the process, what you have learned, and in turn help the organization learn from what went well and what could have gone better.

Now, let's focus on what is meant by "directly and indirectly." In a company such as Interstates, we have an inherent challenge. We have employees all over the country and around the world. Without the opportunity to influence people both directly and indirectly (remotely), we would struggle with creating consistent delivery of our services, and our brand could suffer. Therefore, we have to be able to drive results in many different ways.

One of the ways we drive results is through our EIL programs. Gathering people from all parts of the company and allowing them to experience leadership training in a cohort model pushes results throughout the organization. Participants don't only gain book knowledge; EIL also allows them to build relationships that can then be used to drive results and influence beyond their specific focus areas.

Communication also drives results. As difficult as it often is, we need to continue to be creative in our communication methods and styles. Technology has enabled the use of different methods of communicating, but without intentionality, we will still struggle. We must remember that in-house systems and third-party tools can be of valuable use for communication and can ultimately drive consistent results throughout the organization.

As you can tell, there is no silver bullet. It takes time, energy, and intentionality (not simply activity) to directly and indirectly drive results within the organization. As we continue to grow, this will become even more difficult, but ultimately even more important as we strive to deliver consistently for our clients.

PART THREE
LEADING YOURSELF

Interstates believes in leaders who are lifelong learners. We will never "arrive" as leaders because growing as both a leader and citizen is a lifelong journey. A leader at Interstates takes time to create and follow up on personal and professional goals, displays and promotes a positive attitude, and always stays humble and eager to learn.

CHAPTER NINE

INTERSTATES LEADERS
LIVE WITH PURPOSE

A t work and at home, leaders live with purpose. Purpose is all about our direction and self-awareness. It's about having a North Star to orient and guide us through the critical issues of life: confronting, choosing, pursuing, and facing reality. Living with purpose is also very practical. Imagine a busy employee juggling multiple work responsibilities, parenting their kids, taking care of a home, contributing at church, and volunteering in their community. Leaders do all this without compromising their values, or their sanity, by living with purpose.

At Interstates, leaders align around our common purpose: the importance of the WHY, our vision, servant leadership, and building relationships through our core values. Our leaders believe that when people throughout the organization come together and share in a larger sense of purpose, we are united in a common destiny. We realize a sense of continuity and identity not achievable in any other way.

Within this framework, Interstates leaders find their unique purposes, their personal mission statements, and they coach their people to do the same. Mission statements were discussed broadly in the late '90s during an Interstates-wide discussion of Stephen Covey's excellent book, *The 7 Habits of Highly Effective People.* By 2003, writing personal mission statements had become the norm for EIL 1 attendees. This journey to craft a personal mission statement remains a component of EIL 1 today as one step in the process for participants to understand themselves as individuals on a very personal level.

Writing a mission statement isn't easy, but it is a powerful exercise in taking ownership of your life. Great mission statements are used to make decisions, choose priorities, and guide the leader. A poor mission statement is one that does not get used, even if it sounds awesome. Its application and integration into your life determines if it is a great or poor mission statement. Write a mission statement to express your passion and focus, don't write one to try to impress people.

As you grapple with the career component of your purpose, it's good to consider the following questions:

1. What struggle or sacrifice are you willing to tolerate? It's liberating to realize that everything sucks, some of the time. If you want to be an entrepreneurial leader but you can't handle failure, then you're not going to make it far. If you want to be a big-time project manager but you expect a steady forty-hour week with no surprises, then you're done before you start.

2. What did you do for the sheer joy of it when you were a child? What makes you forget to eat and sleep today? You're looking for the cognitive principles behind activities that enthrall you, e.g., self-competition, passion for improving things,

organizing, generating new ideas, etc. These principles can easily be applied elsewhere.

3. How are you going to save the world? What problems are you uniquely equipped to solve? For example, a friend of mine deeply understands the construction environment and finds purpose in improving the industry via day-to-day operations, challenging clients on the status quo, and contributing at industry conferences. Start saving the world by making a difference where you can.

4. If you were given a one-year sabbatical, what would you do tomorrow? The enemy is complacency. It's critical to understand that passion is the result of action, not the cause of it. If something strikes your interest, write it down, then go out and do it.

Living with purpose is knowing who you are, what your North Star is, how you will make decisions, and what your unique contribution will be. Interstates leaders live authentic lives and serve others. They take Abraham Lincoln's warning seriously:

> *You can fool all the people some of the time and some of the people all the time, but you cannot fool all the people all the time. Regardless of how cleverly you package yourself, others will eventually see through your masquerade and recognize you for what you really are.*

Before that happens, know yourself and your direction.

CHAPTER TEN
INTERSTATES LEADERS DEVELOP THEMSELVES

As our Leadership Model was being developed, the question "Where does personal development start?" was deeply discussed. We wanted to know what base beliefs unleash personal development.

Our self-evaluation concluded that the Senior Leadership team's own development started when we were vulnerable enough to get real and see our own uniqueness – all of our strengths and weaknesses. Being vulnerable allows us to see the reality of our performance, paradigms, and how others see things. This awareness makes clear how desperately we need people around us to constantly help us find and reinforce reality. Reality hunting becomes the duty of leader teams. The more diverse and complementary these people are to the leader's skills, the better.

For these reasons, it is essential that personal development starts with personal discovery, and it is therefore the centerpiece of EIL 1. Get in touch with "you" and figure out how that uniqueness will work in the world around you. After that important (and sometimes painful) step, you are free to always be looking at how to improve, interact better, and have a greater impact on others.

This comes in the form of feedback. Whether offered by others or sought out by you, feedback is the mirror by which to truly see your own performance and impact. Listen carefully and remember that those offering feedback are taking a chance. How you respond to the feedback will dramatically affect how much more information you will get from that person or group.

After achieving awareness and accepting feedback comes the step of choosing. There will always be more things to work on than we can productively focus on at any given moment. After taking inventory of the options, use your intuition and trusted partner feedback to decide on which areas you will begin to work. What will impact others and yourself the most? What seems to be the next step in the journey? Do not wait for others to develop you. A clear identifier of leaders is that they drive their own development and "pull" what they need to succeed in developing themselves. As a word of caution, this development will seldom come solely from training. Although training is helpful for acquiring knowledge, it is not the essence of personal development. Personal development comes from taking risks, trying our new self-awareness and knowledge out in day-to-day practice, and learning how to apply it repeatedly in one continuous learning loop. Training is usually just the beginning of developing a useful skill in your toolbox.

I would encourage you to keep your list of things to work on very short and amp up the intentionality. Meeting a single goal with an intense focus can have a dramatic effect on your progress. If your list is more than one task, don't let it grow past three at one time. It simply dilutes your attention. Never forget that working to leverage your strengths is always more powerful than trying to shore up your weaknesses. For those areas where you struggle, think mitigation. Think about whom to bring around you and complement you. Think about using the team.

The last phase is the sustaining part of development. Remain curious. Reach into the world and see what others are doing and using. Connect some unconventional dots of your own and wonder what they could mean to you or your team. This leads to the most powerful kind of learning and growth. This is a lifetime effort; it must become an integral part of us as leaders – especially at Interstates. As we live out our core WHY, pursuing a better way requires us to be curious, to be open, to learn, and to develop new skills as the challenges of the world unfold.

Personal development is an important piece of leading at Interstates and in the rest of the world. I expect it to be even more so as the world around us changes faster and faster. What people see in you, and how you are leading your own development, inspires them. Share, be transparent, and challenge others to continually seek to be better.

CHAPTER ELEVEN
INTERSTATES LEADERS RELATE WELL WITH OTHERS

Let me start with a question. Whose responsibility is it to relate well with others, the leader's or the other's? I'd like to suggest that, even though both parties have a responsibility, it is up to the leader to take the necessary steps for relating with others. What steps can a leader take to help ensure they are relating well with others?

Build rapport. It takes time and intentionality to build rapport with someone, but through good listening and being approachable you can find commonality that allows individuals to connect. Connecting with someone is very helpful in relating to him or her. Through that connection it is easier to be empathetic when a person is sharing his or her point of view.

Once you have built rapport, a safe environment can be created for people to share their viewpoints, even though they might be different than yours. Seeking out those differing views allows us to think more broadly and possibly achieve a perspective we might not have gotten if we hadn't tried to understand. I had a customer tell me one time, "Think about it until you agree with me." While he was just kidding, that kind of attitude creates an unsafe environment and will shut down opportunities to relate well with others.

Phil Quigley, former CEO of Pacific Bell, once said, "I don't think of leadership as a skill. I think of leadership as a relationship." This attitude allows everyone you work with to feel important and to know his or her opinion is valued and matters. Thinking of leadership as a relationship magnifies the opportunity to draw out the opinions of others and to glean more honest input and feedback than you would have otherwise received.

As a servant leader, one of your responsibilities is to meet others where they are. You may need to modify your typical approach, or at some level even who you are, in order to engage others and relate well with them. Modifying your typical approach takes humility and emotional intelligence. This self-awareness and ability to adapt is crucial for relating well with others.

When I first came to Interstates, Darrel Ramhorst was my supervisor and mentor. I understood computers and programming, but I didn't understand PLCs or electricity. Darrel was a master at coming to my level to teach me what I needed to know to be more effective in my role. With his master's degree in engineering from MIT, it would have been very easy for him to speak well above my head and lose me in the conversation, not to mention cause a great deal of frustration. However, Darrel first determined to understand who I was and where I was. He then adjusted so we could relate at an appropriate level for me to learn and grow in my understanding of the industry. He was a great example for us. My hope is that each of us will do what we can to become better at relating well with others.

CHAPTER TWELVE
INTERSTATES LEADERS MODEL SERVANT LEADERSHIP

Servant leadership is one of Interstates' most important principles, and it's one of the scariest to write about. Why? It's simple: I don't want to be, nor can I be, the poster child for servant leadership. I can't live up to the standard of a servant leader. I will mess up, make mistakes, and become selfish, just to name a few of the reasons.

Modeling servant leadership is a journey, not a destination. That might sound cliché, but if the goal is to be a servant leader, then how others perceive you becomes too important. Your ego becomes the driver, which, in turn, makes you less vulnerable and more self-centered. There is an old saying that warns us if someone says, "Trust me," we should beware. Actions really do speak louder than words.

For me, giving up the finish line of becoming a servant leader was a freeing step. It allowed me to have the right mindset, which includes putting the focus on others, because it isn't about me (or you). It is about helping, serving, and leading others.

Modeling servant leadership has four aspects of equal importance:

1. **Care Genuinely**
   - Show *agape* love, an unconditional love, to all people, but especially to your people.
   - Listen to others in a way that lets them know they've been heard. This empathy shows them they are important and that their ideas matter.
   - Be curious about what is going on with the whole person (professional, personal, wins, struggles, etc.).

2. **Enjoy Serving**
   - Focus on helping, supporting, encouraging, and leading others. You will watch them develop, grow, and succeed. Few things are more rewarding.
   - Enable people to reach new heights by helping them through challenges. You can also help indirectly by offering ideas and suggestions, but not solving problems for them. Remember, as Jim Franken used to say, "Help people help themselves."

3. **Be Approachable and Authentic**
   - Share personal information (beliefs, frustrations, feelings, stories, etc.). This allows others to get to know you and builds strong relationships.
   - Embrace your strengths, weaknesses, mistakes, and goals by sharing them with your team. This transparency will model humility. There's a quote from *The Purpose Driven Life* by Rick Warren that says, "Humility is not thinking less of yourself; it is thinking of yourself less."
   - Have enough self-confidence to ask for others' opinions. Keep this door open so that people are willing to share their ideas with you.

4. **Do the Right Thing**
   - Be a good steward of our people and of the company's resources by making the right decision, which is not always the popular or safe decision.
   - Place the needs (not wants) of others above your own.
   - Although servant leadership is hard, focus on what is best for everyone, and always remember why you're leading.

Many former Interstates leaders have excelled at modeling servant leadership. Darrel Ramhorst was one of those people. He was a quiet leader. Most of the time, he didn't get much attention, and he was okay with that. I was always amazed by how Darrel led. One of his strengths was his ability and desire to teach people and help them grow. His servant leadership took on the form of helping hundreds of people pass journeyman tests or PE exams. People wanted to learn and meet those goals. They knew how much Darrel invested in them and cared about them, and they did not want to let him down.

The best Interstates leaders start with a caring heart and a strong desire to serve others. Learn from them, and then make the journey your own. Remember, servant leadership isn't a status that you achieve. It is a way of doing things that needs to be practiced every day. Enjoy the journey of modeling servant leadership. It will have some highs and lows, but it will be one of the most fulfilling journeys you'll ever experience. Choose to lead The Interstates Way by modeling servant leadership today, and then choose to do it again tomorrow.

PART FOUR
SERVING CLIENTS

S erving clients is at the heart of our business and the desire to make a difference for our clients and business partners is the very essence of what it is to lead at Interstates. Without great client relationships, Interstates simply cannot prosper. This is why serving clients must remain our highest priority.

CHAPTER THIRTEEN
INTERSTATES LEADERS BUILD CLIENT RELATIONSHIPS

Building strong client relationships doesn't simply mean being buddy-buddy with them. Neither does it mean manipulating a situation and relationship for our benefit. It is really about living our core values of "Building relationships through: Dependability, Integrity, Trust, Quality, and Family." We want all Interstates leaders to develop well-rounded client relationships.

These relationships are:

- Mutually beneficial: It's good for the client and good for Interstates.
- Professional: We are viewed as a company (and individuals) with credibility, and clients have confidence in us to deliver the results they need.
- Personal: We are connecting to and/or know the individuals outside of work.

Applying servant leadership to client relationships is also important. We need to treat our clients with respect, regardless of their titles or positions. Looking for ways to make a difference and add value for our clients is key. This could be in the form of passing an interesting article on to them, asking for their feedback, or asking hard questions that might challenge some of their assumptions. There are a lot of examples that would fit here, but I wanted to share just a couple:

AGP

Randy Van Voorst and Larry Den Herder have great relationships with several key leaders at AGP. The strength of those relationships allows Randy and Larry to ask harder questions and push AGP for clarity on projects without the fear of losing the client. In fact, AGP has come to expect that push and those questions because they know the intent for them is to make their organization and projects better. As the years have gone on, Randy and Larry have become close friends with that group. They get together for professional and personal events (hunting, fishing, golfing, etc.). Larry and Randy were invited to celebrate with a couple of retiring AGP leaders, which is significant considering most of the other attendees were AGP team members. That's a testament to the depth of their connection. This type of relationship allows them to be direct, vulnerable, resolve issues faster, and most importantly, serve the client better.

ARDENT MILLS

Jake Ten Haken, Michael De Boer, and Bryan Monroe also have awesome relationships with the team at Ardent Mills. They talk, text, and email frequently. Sometimes it's about work and sometimes about their skills (or lack of) related to maneuvering a snowmobile. If you catch the beginning of an Ardent Mills meeting or phone call, you're likely to hear some trash talk. However, at the end of the day, the team from Ardent Mills knows and trusts these guys at a deep level. Developing these friendships and building trust has led to many successful projects for these teams.

You never know how strong a relationship is until it is tested. Therefore, when you face a tough situation with a client, it is really an opportunity for you to show the client what great client relationships really mean. Resolving tough situations by walking with them as a partner will always deepen a relationship. This does not mean to roll over, but it does mean to do the right thing! Be up front, be direct, be helpful, and be a partner to them. That's how you build client relationships The Interstates Way.

CHAPTER FOURTEEN
INTERSTATES LEADERS ADVOCATE FOR THE CLIENT

A dictionary might define an advocate as someone who openly supports and recommends another individual, group, or policy. Client advocates represent the customer to the rest of Interstates. All leaders can advocate for our clients; you don't have to be in operations or doing project delivery. Leaders must keep our culture centered on serving others. They ensure training and accountability on client service expectations and can also develop systems and processes to better serve our clients. For example, categorizing client account types through the Client Perspective process in 2015 helped to clarify who is responsible for which clients, aligned business development and operations around common clients, and provided a framework for setting goals and utilizing resources to better serve various client types.

Leaders who advocate for the client regularly walk beside project teams to help them understand a client's business goals for the projects they have entrusted to us. After all, whether a new grain export facility is justified based on receiving grain by the next harvest or on the premise of increasing long-term market share can have a drastic impact on how we manage the construction schedule.

During the difficulties and surprises of project work, client advocates keep Interstates' people focused on the client's needs and point-of-view. Project work is stressful, and personalities can clash. Client-focused leaders remind project teams of the client's importance and focus them on the positive aspects of the client. They promote the importance of client relationships lasting beyond any single project.

Client advocates understand how Interstates' design-build value proposition – Rapid project delivery, Innovative solutions, Single-source responsibility, and Early dependable pricing (RISE) – can benefit our clients. In the late '90s, an Interstates proposal team exemplified RISE and secured a large sugar facility project in Moses Lake, Washington, that enabled us to help the client, stretch our people, and grow Interstates to a new level.

This client had been unsuccessful in getting its project funded. Our proposal leaders quickly understood that the complex plans and design-bid format were driving up the client's costs and extending its schedule. After explaining the RISE benefits of a design-build project to the client and sharing the reduced budget that we agreed to stand behind, the client was able to get the project approved and moving forward, trusting our early, dependable pricing and our ability to speed up the pace of the project.

Another great example, the AGP account team has developed several key ways to advocate for this specific client. As we've grown with this important all-star client over the last twenty+ years, a number of characteristics illustrate what client advocacy is all about:

- We have built a strong working relationship with AGP. We're fully zippered – multiple people at Interstates have relationships with people at multiple levels at AGP.
- We're at the planning table early on in projects, understanding AGP's goals and business needs. Randy Van Voorst, our account leader (and one of AGP's biggest advocates) is closely involved with multiple AGP leaders in budgeting their projects long before board approval.
- We've dedicated a tailored, multi-service team to serve AGP, and all departments know that serving them well is a priority.
- We know the facilities' electrical systems inside and out. This enables us to be their trusted advisors.

Advocating for a client is all about developing an account team tailored to the client's specific needs, a team that passionately and intentionally serves the customer. A service culture doesn't happen by accident. Rather, it is a reflection of the group's leadership. Their attitudes, their values, and their commitment to service excellence will drive the actions of others in the organization. Always has, always will. Know how you are "making a difference for your clients" and continue leading The Interstates Way by advocating for the client!

CHAPTER FIFTEEN
INTERSTATES LEADERS BALANCE CLIENT NEEDS WITH INTERNAL PROCESSES

It's not uncommon for leaders in our organization to have a lengthy tenure with the company; I have been with Interstates for nearly twenty-two years. During that time, many things have changed, including our clients' needs. When I started, it seemed as though we had more lead time to plan and prepare, more construction time to accomplish the work on site, and more time to get a plant up and running. Today our clients feel the pressure to produce sooner, more consistently, with higher quality, and with better controls.

Interstates has adapted a lot over the years as well. Our internal tools and processes have continued to evolve and develop, allowing us to become industry leaders in a design-build methodology that meets the demands of our client base while adding unique value.

If you think things haven't changed that much in the past twenty years, spend a little time reflecting on what life was like in 1994. You were excited to have just acquired your first plain paper fax machine, your mobile phone weighed several pounds, if you had one, and Al Gore was still in the process of inventing the Internet.

You probably didn't have an individual email address and if you had a personal computer at home, you were one of the first.

While many things have changed, the need to communicate with our clients and understand their needs, and then match that understanding with how we deliver results, has not changed. Early in the discovery phase of a project, it is important to understand both what the client wants as a final result of the project and what is important to the client during the project. Because we are an integral part of helping our clients achieve their goals, this process is critical to their success.

The discovery process uncovers unique things the client wants to accomplish and why those goals are important. It helps us to understand what might be negotiable and what is not. And we can ask, "Are there other ways to achieve the same desired results?" Through the discovery process we determine if we have the tools, systems, capabilities, and resources to help them meet their objectives.

Most often, we find that the systems and tools we have in place do meet the needs of the client. Through creativity and adaptation of what we already have in place, flexibility allows us to deliver the specific and unique requests of our clients. However, if through the discovery process we determine we can't deliver what the client wants, we may have to help them find another way. We have to continually balance the needs of our clients with the capabilities of our internal processes. We need to make adjustments as the market changes, but we can't be all things to all people all the time. Creativity, understanding our clients' needs, and matching our unique abilities to the attributes that allow our clients to succeed will win every time.

CHAPTER SIXTEEN
INTERSTATES LEADERS NETWORK WITHIN OUR INDUSTRY

Networking within our industry is a way to serve clients. This may seem like an odd statement. It struck me as odd, too, when the Senior Leaders worked through selecting the essential elements of The Leadership Model for Interstates. Why did we include this? The answer is found deep in our culture. At our core, we are experts. We are proud of our ability to really know the ins and outs of the industries in which we participate. We strongly connect what we know to what we are able to offer the client in terms of expert advice.

To be experts at the trusted advisor level, we need to know what is happening in our industries. What are the issues challenging the businesses we are trying to support? It may not matter that it has little to do with electrical engineering or construction. To get in touch with this kind of information we must get both a broad and deep understanding of the issues. When we do, we can become trusted advisors for our clients.

You see, networking by definition is building relationships. As in our core values statement: Building relationships through: Dependability, Integrity, Trust, Quality, and Family. The key idea here, and what we sometimes miss when discussing our core values, is the building relationships component. To build effective relationships, we need to know about clients' problems, challenges, and big opportunities. In other words, networking provides many of the seeds we use to develop our client relationships.

This takes an investment. Sometimes it's time and travel. Sometimes it's sponsorship. Nevertheless, it is essential that networking happen. When we are out there networking we hear what is happening; we interact with clients and can test assumptions and listen for opportunities to serve. If we were Navy SEALS, it would be reconnaissance for our mission of serving our clients. In addition, when clients see us contributing to their industries, they see us as being in it with them. This is an important perception to maintain when trying to connect with clients.

A final word on networking: The information gathered must be processed and shared to be effective. We cannot afford networking to be limited to socializing and cocktails without follow-up or intentionality. Information gathered needs to be synthesized with other conversations and discussed in a forum with others so that it will allow us to react, to offer assistance, and to change our approach. This may be one of the more difficult parts of networking, as opportunities seldom present themselves plainly as, "We need to do XYZ."

Even though the challenges around networking are substantial, the need for networking is great. It is truly a key element of leading at Interstates.

PART FIVE
LEADING PEOPLE

At Interstates, we believe that anyone can be a leader, regardless of position, by first being a servant. True leaders surround themselves with talented and motivated individuals and equip those on their team for success. This is done through coaching, mentorship, developing deep relationships with our peers, and having clear communication through the valuable gift of feedback.

CHAPTER SEVENTEEN
INTERSTATES LEADERS COMMUNICATE EFFECTIVELY

D o you know how much pressure there is in writing about effective communication? How ironic is it that we need to communicate about communication? Communication is so basic and yet so critical in everything that we do. Often, when troubles arise, we can boil them down to poor communication.

You have heard the saying, "It takes two to tango." Well, the same holds true for communication: it takes two. Successful communication only occurs when something has been shared and its meaning has been received. It doesn't matter if that communication is spoken, written, in a PowerPoint presentation, in a video, or otherwise. If the meaning of the message is not received, successful communication hasn't happened. So whose responsibility is it to ensure successful communication? Leaders think about successful communication in two ways – giving and receiving. We often think of the giver as having the majority of the responsibility in communication. While that is critical, the receiver also plays a major role.

Let's first discuss receiving. Receiving, or listening, is active. You need to be fully engaged, seeking to understand the meaning of what is being shared. Don't forget that as leaders we need to keep the environment safe for those who are sharing. Sometimes this takes patience. Sometimes it takes self-control. There may be times when we don't agree with what is being said, but, nonetheless, we have an obligation to actively listen and make sure people know they have been heard. There are several techniques for making sure you have heard the true intent of what has been shared. One example is to repeat back, in your own words, what you have heard. Of course, not all forms of communication allow this kind of interaction, but active listening to any form of medium requires your full attention.

The other responsibility in effectively communicating is giving or sharing information. I have had to remind myself multiple times that "just because I said it, doesn't mean they heard it." In order to share information appropriately, you have to know your audience and tailor the delivery of information to communicate effectively with them. You may have to say it in multiple ways, multiple times, and in different styles to be sure the message is being received. It might even be wise to ask someone what they have heard so you can confirm that the message you shared has been fully transmitted.

Not only is it the responsibility of the leader to share information in an understandable and concise way, it is also our duty to be wise about what information is being shared. As a leader, you need to discern what information and how much information is appropriate to be shared with your audience. An example might be when making a change in the organization. The manager above you may only need to know the reason or the "why" for the change. Your subordinates not only need to know the "why" but also the "how" to implement the change. The same information may need to be shared differently, or not at all, with different audiences. As a leader, making this determination can be a challenge, especially when you are dealing with multiple generations that want and expect different levels of information.

While communication happens every day in a myriad of ways, it is not always effective or appropriate. As a leader, you have a great responsibility in making sure you can understand the message given to you as well as sharing the appropriate amount of information in an understandable way to diverse groups of people.

CHAPTER EIGHTEEN
INTERSTATES LEADERS DEVELOP, COACH, AND MOTIVATE

During most EIL1 classes, we ask two very telling questions:

1. Who was the best supervisor/leader you have ever had, and why?
2. Who was the worst supervisor/leader you have ever had, and why?

The answer to the first question revolves around development, coaching and motivation. Most of the time, the leader that tops the best list focused on helping the person grow, elevate their performance, or achieve more than the employee thought was possible. They played the role of a mentor, coach, cheerleader, etc. Their goals were balanced between getting things done and positioning other people to learn and grow.

The answer to the second question is also interesting. Leaders on the worst list are focused on themselves and getting things done. They treat their people as tools. I have had many people from the Interstates family invest their time in me to help me grow. For example:

- Jim Franken coached and pushed me about leadership and being forward thinking.
- Darrel Ramhorst gave me hard feedback, pushed me to have high standards, and encouraged me when I needed it.
- John DeZeeuw helped me understand the business of construction, engineering, and automation. He also inspired me to have a balanced perspective, one where I balanced the needs of the employees, the needs of the clients, and the needs of the business.
- Larry Den Herder focused on providing feedback and direction on how to make a difference for our clients.
- Jack Woelber provides great feedback and support. He also helps reinforce the desire to build a great culture, live our core values, and provide opportunities for people.
- Dave Crumrine helps me to think broadly and deeply about our clients and our business. His ideas, feedback, and passion about pursuing a better way have raised the expectations of our team.
- Doug Post encourages me to be a better systems thinker and to constantly read and look for solutions for our teams and for our clients.
- Others in our organization have also helped by committing to provide me great feedback, insight, and perspective to help me grow as a leader.

As you think about how to develop, coach, and motivate your team, there are two approaches that are effective. If you want to have amazing results, the key is to implement them together. These approaches are:

1. Planned Development: As a leader, know your team. Know what they want to develop and support their efforts. You should also have open and candid conversations with them about what they need to develop and why. As you get to know them you'll find out what they need, e.g., skill development, experience, self-awareness, confidence, etc.

2. Teachable Moments: These moments pop up every day, but many of them go unnoticed. A great leader has the ability to see them and leverage them. They may not see 100 percent of them; it may be more like baseball where hitting .300 is considered great. They connect the teachable moment with the development that employee needs at that time. This is incredibly powerful when it happens and can really motivate both the employee and the leader.

Interstates excels at development, both on the technical side and on the leadership side. Your responsibility, your opportunity, your privilege is investing some of yourself into your team, your peers, and other leaders to help them reach their potential. When it happens, we create a win-win situation. When you invest in people, you are leading The Interstates Way!

CHAPTER NINETEEN
INTERSTATES LEADERS ATTRACT, HIRE, AND RETAIN TALENT

I once thought attracting, hiring, and retaining employees was the job of the Human Resources department. Wrong! This element of leadership is so important that it was one of the first ones the Senior Team picked when putting together our Leadership Model. You see, almost all of the other pieces of the Leadership Model are unable to start without the team. You have to get and keep a core team to even begin leading. Aside from some trucks, tools, and computers that anyone could buy, we are a people company, pure and simple. The intellectual property we have developed and hold resides mostly within our people.

As a leader this needs to be crystal clear to you. You need to make sure your team is being identified, grown, and retained. This is a constant process you must execute as a leader. HR will be of great assistance to you, but you cannot delegate this responsibility away. Developing your talent is fundamental to leadership!

The HR department, and anyone else in the potential workforce, will be happy to tell you that people want to sign up for a cause or a mission, not just a job. Generationally, this is truer today than ever before. In trying to find out what an employer is about, prospective employees want to hear from the leaders of the cause. They want to be inspired. They want to see it. They want to feel it when they are interviewing and interacting with us. When you are recruiting team members, you should think of it as high-stakes deal making. Candidates are offering part of their lives, and you are offering part of your business. This may be one of the biggest win-win setups of all time, and it has high stakes. That's why leaders must be deeply into the talent game.

Once on the team, members want to be taught, challenged, and energized. We have started referring to this as employee engagement. This requires leadership, and a lot of it. Whether this leadership comes from front-line supervision, middle management, or the top tier, it doesn't matter. The team needs it, and the business depends on it. The difference between an engaged team and a disengaged team could very well be the success or failure of the entire business.

Now for the good news. With the right philosophy and intent, growing your talent pool can be one of the most energizing and rewarding parts of your job. Finding and nurturing a great team provides a feeling for leaders unlike many others and can last for a lifetime. Doing these things well becomes a gift that keeps on giving, both for the organization and the individuals involved. Leaders often talk about their greatest achievements being the people they helped bring up and grow. Those brought up often think of their leaders and mentors as family long after the direct work is done. This can be a great way for the servant leader's heart to really shine through.

Interstates has a rich history of cultivating people from varied backgrounds and stories into successful, long-term team members. It takes intentional work by leaders, but there is no more foundational thing in a business than building the talent.

CHAPTER TWENTY

INTERSTATES LEADERS FOSTER PRODUCTIVE INTERNAL RELATIONSHIPS

Have you ever heard the phrase, "A leader with no followers is really just a person out for a walk?" How is it that some leaders seem to have a lot of influence and others struggle to maintain even a little? Why is it that when some folks want to implement a change, it comes so much easier for them than it might be for others? Why do some people seem to get buy-in for an idea so much more quickly than others? There are a lot of answers to those questions, but an overarching reason can be found in the importance of having relationships.

Relationships inside an organization are important for numerous reasons. First, most people enjoy their jobs more if they have productive relationships at work. Work is more gratifying and fulfilling when people interact. Individuals have a sense of belonging through relationships, which gives them more job satisfaction. Second, when you build relationships, you are investing in others, and they in you. This mutual investment should create a mutual benefit. Through that mutual benefit, people can win together and share each other's successes as well as the success of the team.

In chapter 8, we discuss being able to drive results directly and indirectly. Relationships offer significant benefits when you are trying to drive results indirectly, both in your area of business as well as across other divisions or business units. Through the relationships we've purposefully built with others, we can indirectly drive results. Without those relationships, this indirect influence is incredibly difficult to achieve.

How can you build those internal relationships? It may seem very basic, but you must be willing to initiate conversation and dialogue. We get to know each other through communication. It doesn't happen overnight. After all, you didn't become best friends with anyone the first time you visited. It took time. But over time, through ongoing conversations, shared experiences, and successes or hardships, the relationship grew and became what it is today. Strong relationships allow for open and honest dialogue. These intentionally built relationships offer permission to give and receive feedback, creating a culture of honesty and helping each other for mutual benefit. In the end, everyone wins.

So, while some of us may tend to keep to ourselves and do our own thing, it is important as leaders that we build relationships within our teams and across the organization. Not only will building relationships help you and others lead, these relationships will also provide more enjoyable and meaningful interactions every day.

CHAPTER TWENTY-ONE
INTERSTATES LEADERS DO TOUGH CONVERSATIONS WELL

"I love having tough conversations! They are fun and exciting!" said no one ever.

Having tough conversations with your direct reports, peers, clients and supervisors is hard, no doubt. As a leader, having those tough conversations and doing them well is also one of your most important responsibilities.

Why is it so important?

- It is one of the best ways to align people and teams.
- It builds trust since people know they can talk to you about anything and that you really want them to succeed.
- It sets the stage for a healthy and productive culture.
- Because not having tough conversations is the most common cause of leadership failures.

Three tips for how to do tough conversations well:

1. Show high EQ (Emotional Intelligence).
2. Lean in.
3. Stay in the "sweet spot" during the conversation.

EQ

Emotional Intelligence is defined as knowing how you and others feel and what to do about it to achieve a successful and positive result. Here are the four main components and how you can leverage them to help you prepare for productive tough conversations:

1. Self-Awareness. On a regular basis, identify your hot buttons (topics, issues, or people) and know your emotions around them. It's important to be honest with yourself.
2. Self-Management. Calm is contagious, so manage and control your emotions to prepare yourself to aim your responses in a positive direction, not a judgmental way.
3. Social Awareness. Pick up on the other person's emotions in order to understand what he or she is thinking and feeling.
4. Social/Relationship Management. Using all of the above information, talk about the issue in a productive way.

LEAN IN

This one is simple – just do it! Take time to prepare for the tough conversation and assume the best about the other person. During the conversation, stay in the final element, the sweet spot.

SWEET SPOT

During the stress of a tough conversation, we have a tendency to fall into one of two categories: fight or flight.

- When we go into fight mode, we want to convince the other person that they are wrong and we are right. We forget to listen, and we become judgmental.
- When we go into flight mode, we want to avoid the situation or get out of it as quickly as possible. We do not state our thoughts or opinions.

The sweet spot. This is when we get it right. We use high EQ and we lean in to those tough conversations. We find a good balance of being curious and being candid, and this is how we overcome falling into those fight or flight categories.

1. If you are a fighter, take time to ask questions, listen to the answers, and show empathy. Be curious.
2. If you are a flighter (yes, I'm making up words), take a chance by sharing your honest thoughts and opinions without feeling like you have to prove yourself. Be candid.

Tough conversations can be a mixed bag. Stay in the sweet spot by being curious and truly believing the best of people even though most of us don't like having these conversations. They are often the source of great stress. Over the years I have learned to recognize that stress as a signal; a signal to lean into the tough conversation. Don't avoid it. For the most part these conversations are a relief to both people because participants often have similar concerns and emotions. Just getting the topic on the table is a big step and a win.

If we can have productive tough conversations, we will be leading The Interstates Way!

CONCLUSION:
CHALLENGE TO KEEP LEADING
THE INTERSTATES WAY

During the process of reading this book, hopefully you have reflected on your role in providing and developing leadership. So, now it is your turn and your decision. Are you going to leverage this information and apply it, or not? Are you going to assess your strengths and acknowledge your weaknesses, or not? Are you going to take time to develop yourself and others, or not? The choice has always been, and will always be, yours.

As you make these decisions, please consider:

1. You are ridiculously in charge of your leadership development and your team's development.
2. "Live as if you were to die tomorrow. Learn as if you were to live forever." – Mahatma Gandhi.

Our hope is that you will be the kind of leader who will invest in yourself and others. The kind of leader who won't defer, but will take the initiative and risk to lead.

We want you to:

- Live it
- Own it
- Teach it

That is leading The Interstates Way!

CONTRIBUTORS

AUTHORS:

- Scott Peterson – CEO
- Jack Woelber – President – Interstates Control Systems
- Dave Crumrine – President – Interstates Construction
- Doug Post – President – Interstates Engineering

EIL CLASS SPONSORS
BOOK TEAM:

- Daren Dieleman – Director of Project Delivery – ICSI
- Blair Harp – Asset Manager
- Jaron VandeHoef – Business Development Principal – IE
- Reid Vander Veen – Director of Marketing and Communications

TOOL KIT TEAM:

- Dave Eekhoff – Chief Estimator – IC
- Mike Meyers – Chief Information Officer
- Dave Taylor – Director of Planning and Prefab
- Joel Van Egdom – Director of Strategy and Support

IMPLEMENTATION TEAM:

- Catherine Bloom – Chief Financial Officer
- Doug Brunsting – Director of Regional Offices
- Christina Cota – Director of Human Resources
- Eric Van Den Berg – Operations Manager – IE
- Marty Van Der Sloot – Division Manager – MIT

ACKNOWLEDGEMENTS:

We would like to recognize and thank Vanessa Kiley and Sara Den Bestin. They provided an outside perspective, while pushing the Senior Team to reflect, think, show passion, and to listen. Their input, feedback, and guidance had a huge impact on us as individuals, as a team, and on the Leadership Model.

A big thank you goes out to all others who have supported the efforts of generating content for the blog and this book. Many individuals have had an impact on this book or the original blog content in various ways. Some of those individuals include: Kristi Segar, Lori Van Beek, David Krahling, Joanna Van Velzen, Jodi Acres, Jessica De Boom, and Jenna Aker.

Special thanks also goes out to Tom Morgan whose assistance greatly enhanced the experience of the EIL 3 peer group during the download of the Leadership Model from our Senior Leadership team.

We also would like to acknowledge the team at Throne Publishing, in particular Jordan Loftis and Jeremy Brown. Your team has been instrumental in the process of bringing the idea for this book from concept to completion.

Finally, we would like to thank all the past and current team members and leaders of Interstates. Our culture and our success all comes from you. You are what makes Interstates an amazing place.

Continue leading The Interstates Way.